JOHN STEINBECK

JOHN STEINBECK

A. Susan Williams

Life and Works

Jane Austen
The Brontës
Joseph Conrad
Charles Dickens
T. S. Eliot
Thomas Hardy
Hemingway
D. H. Lawrence
Katherine Mansfield
George Orwell
Shakespeare
John Steinbeck
H. G. Wells
Virginia Woolf

Cover illustration by David Armitage

First published in 1990 by
Wayland (Publishers) Ltd
61 Western Road, Hove
East Sussex BN3 1JD, England

© Copyright 1990 Wayland (Publishers) Ltd

Series adviser: Dr Cornelia Cook
Series designer: David Armitage
Editor: Susannah Foreman

British Library Cataloguing in Publication Data
Williams, A. Susan
    John Steinbeck, A. Susan Williams. – (Life and works)
    I. Title II. Series
    813″.52

    ISBN 1–85210–841–X

Typeset by Rachel Gibbs, Wayland
Printed in Italy by G. Canale & C.S.p.A., Turin
Bound in the UK by Maclehose & Partners, Portsmouth

Contents

1 John Steinbeck's Life, 1902–1968

A Californian childhood

Throughout his life, John Steinbeck treasured his recollections of growing up in California. He spent his youth roaming the fertile Salinas Valley, which was bounded by mountains on two sides and by the Pacific Ocean at one end. 'I remember my childhood names for grasses and secret flowers,' he writes in *East of Eden*. 'I remember where a toad may live and what time the birds awaken in the summer – and what trees and seasons smelled like – how people looked and walked and smelled even.' So powerful were his memories that Steinbeck set twelve of his seventeen novels in the state of California.

He was born on 27 February 1902 in Salinas, which is now a modern city but was then a small country town. He lived there with his parents and three sisters until he was 19. In the summer, the family escaped from the heat of the town to a cottage near the ocean. The Steinbecks were a respected family in the Salinas community. John Steinbeck Senior managed his own feed and grain store and for many years was the treasurer of Monterey County. His wife, Olive Hamilton, had been a schoolteacher before her children were born, and was admired as a wise and cultured woman.

She liked to coddle John, saying he needed special attention because he was sensitive and clever. This annoyed John's father, who tried to weaken his wife's

Opposite John Steinbeck as a boy of five. He is standing in the garden of his family's home in the town of Salinas, California.

6

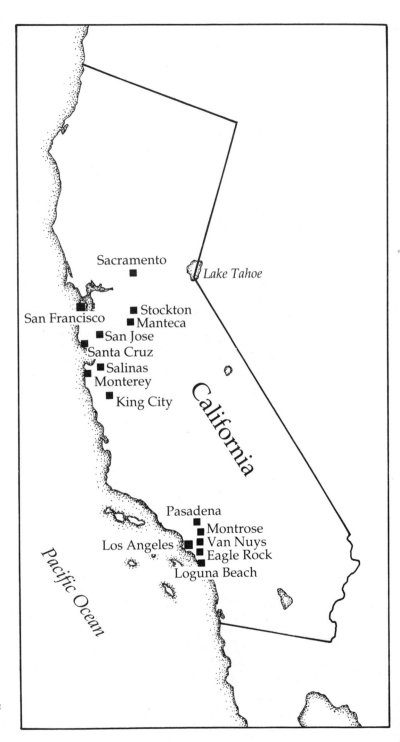

Sacramento

■ Lake Tahoe

■ Stockton

■ Manteca

San Francisco

■ San Jose

Santa Cruz

■ Salinas

Monterey

■ King City

California

Pasadena

■ Montrose

■ Van Nuys

Los Angeles

Eagle Rock

Loguna Beach

Pacific Ocean

A map of California, the state in which Steinbeck was born and grew up. It is the setting for most of his major fiction.

John Steinbeck's mother, Olive Hamilton. Like the schoolteacher of the same name in East of Eden, 'She was loving and firm with her family, three girls and me, trained us to housework . . . and manners. When angered she had a terrible eye . . . '

influence by impressing on his son the need to become a responsible adult. John reacted to this confusing mixture of expectations by being a difficult child. A neighbour thought that he was 'rotten-spoiled . . . an overgrown kid with a big belly.' In fact, though, he was often miserable. 'I remember the sorrow at not being part of things in my childhood,' he remarked forty or so years later. 'Something cut me off always.'

John Steinbeck Senior, on the day of his wedding in 1890 to Olive Hamilton. His son John called him 'a good and a strong man'.

Study and work

John did well at Salinas High School and was a keen reporter for the school newspaper. In 1920, at the age of 19, he went to Stanford University to study English. But after five years at university, he dropped out without a degree. He was certainly clever enough, but could not see the point of studying his course material. His favourite activity at Stanford was the English Club, where students and teachers met to share their literary interests. Steinbeck's enthusiasm for the club put other students off. 'A fellow named Steinbeck,' another student was warned,

The Steinbeck family on a picnic by the sea in 1904, when John was an infant of two.

'comes to every meeting and insists on reading his stuff to
everyone.'

Steinbeck probably got more education from his
holiday jobs than from his formal education. He worked
at different times as a shop attendant, as a labourer, as a
caretaker, as a fruit-picker, as a carpenter, on a road gang,
in a sugar-beet factory and on ranches. While he was a
university student, he spent his vacations working on a

ranch for the Spreckels Sugar Company. His depiction of life as a ranch hand in *Of Mice and Men* owes much to this job.

In 1925, after leaving Stanford, Steinbeck went to New York. He hoped this move to the big city would be good for his writing. He was pleased to get work as a labourer building the Madison Square Gardens, but found the work exhausting. Then an uncle found him a job on a magazine

Steinbeck's first wife, Carol Henning, who married him in 1930. They divorced twelve years later because John felt trapped by the marriage.

called the *American*, but it did not last very long. Steinbeck did not like the people he met at the magazine office, who reminded him of the intellectuals and cultured middle classes that he had despised at Stanford (the 'shit-heels' of *The Grapes of Wrath*). He realized that he much preferred the company of working men and women. We see this preference in his fiction, where labourers, small farmers, prostitutes and outcasts are the most likeable of all his characters.

Marriage and divorce

Steinbeck's first two marriages ended in divorce. The major difficulties in these marriages arose from his fears of settling down. *Cannery Row* reveals his horror of domesticity and of the influence of women. When Mack and some of the 'boys' from Cannery Row hunt for frogs along the river, the owner of the land invites them home. The house is very untidy, we are told, because the man's wife is away. Steinbeck then draws a contrast between the oppressive influence of women and the relaxed companionship of men. The boys, he says,

> were unconsciously glad [the wife] wasn't there. The kind of woman who put paper on shelves and had little towels like that instinctively distrusted Mack and the boys. Such women knew that they were the worst threats to a home, for they offered ease and thought and companionship as opposed to neatness, order, and properness. They were very glad she was away.

At first, Steinbeck was happy with his first wife, Carol Henning, whom he married in 1930. His father provided them with an allowance and a little cottage in Pacific Grove, so that John would have the freedom to write. The allowance was small, but this had the advantage for John of removing the threat of domestic ease. In any case, Carol applied her usual good humour to the problem of money. Like Mary Talbot in *Cannery Row*, she cut pictures of appetising food out of magazines and spread the table with these paper delicacies! Carol helped John with his writing by spending long hours typing his manuscripts.

Problems developed in the marriage when John's earnings started to increase. Carol was delighted and lost no time in making plans to be more comfortable. John was

Opposite
Gwyndolyn Conger, with whom John fell in love while he was still married to Carol. They married in 1943 and had two sons. This second marriage also ended in divorce.

14

dismayed by this prospect of settling down to respectability. He felt very distant from Carol and they had more and more quarrels. In 1940, he fell in love with Gwyndolyn Conger, a dancer.

He separated from Carol in 1941. She tried hard to win him back, but they were eventually divorced in 1942. John married Gwyn in 1943 and at first they were happy. But soon, the same sort of conflicts developed. Gwyn wanted to settle down, but John was still hankering for freedom and adventure. When he went to Europe as a journalist during the Second World War, Gwyn felt lonely and miserable, and started to drink too much alcohol. After his return, they had two sons – Thom in 1944 and John in 1946. But Gwyn still felt neglected by her husband. In 1948, she left him.

John was devastated. He developed an intense dislike for women, avoiding them whenever possible. He remarked during this period that American women 'are trained by their mothers in a contempt for men and so they compete with men . . . The American girl makes a servant of her husband and then finds him contemptible for being a servant.' As a woman working at the office of his literary agent observed, he had 'very peculiar ideas of women these days.'

Steinbeck found it almost as difficult to be a father as he did to be a husband. When his sons were little, their natural inability to talk sensibly made him impatient. He would 'have preferred that both the boys had been born age twelve,' writes one biographer. But he felt a genuine concern for them. He was always making plans for them, usually with a view to turning them into 'men'. Not long after breaking up with Gwyn, he wrote to a friend that, 'I have my boys the two months this summer and I am going to give them some manness – by that I mean they are going to help me do things, physical things, they are going to be let to wander if they want.' He added that:

> They can have hammers and nails and boxes to build with. Thom is old enough to take the dual control of an airplane so can learn to fly as he learned to talk with an automatic reflex sense. And he can drive my jeep on country roads.

Since Thom was only five years old at this time, Steinbeck's understanding of the needs of a child must have been very limited!

Opposite *John Steinbeck on holiday with his two sons, Thom and John IV. He found it hard to be a father because he could not understand the needs of small children.*

Elaine and John Steinbeck. John loved his third wife so much that he 'would go to any length to withhold from her any pain or sorrow that is not needful for her own enrichment'.

Opposite *Elaine Scott and John Steinbeck at their wedding reception in 1950. This marriage was a happy one and lasted until his death in 1968.*

A third and happy marriage

As Steinbeck started to recover from the breakdown of his marriage to Gwyn, he remarked that, 'the difficulty of course is that I like women. It is only wives I am in trouble with.' Then he met and fell in love with Elaine Scott, who was already married. He began to hope that if Elaine were able to get a divorce, he would enjoy being married to her. 'Both of my wives were somehow in competition with me,' he explained. 'I was ashamed of being noticed. I am not a bit ashamed now. Elaine is on *my* side, not against me. The result is that I am more relaxed than I have ever been.'

The couple married in 1950, when John was 48. Elaine ensured that he had ample freedom, so he did not feel tied down. They enjoyed eighteen years together until John died on 20 December 1968. Shortly before his death, he wrote that, 'I love Elaine more than myself. Her well being and comfort and happiness are more important than my own.'

The Great Depression

24 October, 1929 was a day that is thought of with horror by Americans. On this 'Black Thursday', as it came to be called, a wave of panic selling of stocks swept the New York Stock Exchange, which provoked a collapse of share

Panic on Wall Street in New York on 29 October 1929, the day of the Wall Street Crash. Millions of dollars were wiped off share values in a few hours, which provoked a world economic crisis called the Great Depression.

and other security prices. This in turn caused the economic collapse known as the Great Depression, which lasted roughly from 1930 until the USA's entry into the Second World War in 1941. By 1932, over 100,000 businesses and thousands of banks had failed, so that many Americans

The shantytowns of the Depression were called Hoovervilles.

Opposite *Franklin D. Roosevelt, who became President of the USA in the middle of the Depression. He tried to help the poor with a programme of reforms called the New Deal.*

lost all their money. It was an economic and a human disaster. In the worst years of the Depression, more than a quarter of the labour force was unemployed.

It is hard today to imagine the misery suffered by the victims of the Depression. There was no welfare, no social security and hardly any help from the state. Thousands of families had little to eat and nowhere to live except cardboard boxes and derelict cars in shanty towns called 'Hoovervilles' (named after Herbert C. Hoover, the President of the USA until 1932).

In the 1932 elections, Franklin D. Roosevelt, a Democrat, was elected President on the basis of his promise of a 'New Deal' for the American people. He was full of good ideas to rescue people from poverty, inspiring public confidence with the famous statement that, 'The only thing we have to fear is fear itself'. In accordance with the 'New Deal', a Works Progress Administration was set up to provide

work and pay for those who were out of work, pensions for the old and unemployed, and laws to assist the recovery of the economy. But even Roosevelt's efforts could not end the Depression. It was only when the USA entered the Second World War, creating jobs for the unemployed and boosting economic growth, that the American people could see their way out of the Depression.

The Dust Bowl and the exodus of the 'Okies'

Traditional farming life was devastated by the Depression. Small farmers and sharecroppers were driven off their land by the banks, because they could not repay their bank loans. In Oklahoma, Arkansas and some nearby states, the banks and large corporations sent tractors to sweep through the farms and houses that now belonged to them. The situation was made even worse by a terrible drought and persistent winds that took the topsoil off millions of acres of farmland. This created a vast desert area that came to be known as the Dust Bowl. It was the final disaster in the lives of many small farmers who had been trying to stay on their land. Like the Joads in *The Grapes of Wrath*, they were forced to abandon their homes and way of life.

By 1930, thousands of people were heading away from the storms of the Dust Bowl to California in the west. By the time Steinbeck was writing *The Grapes of Wrath* in 1938:

> A half-million people [were] moving over the country; a million more restive, ready to move; ten million more feeling the first nervousness.

The migrants hoped to find a job or a piece of land in California. Grampa Joad's pledge that when he got to California, he would 'pick me a wash tub full a grapes, an' I'm gonna set in em, an' scrooge aroun', an' let the juice run down my pants', was typical of the migrants' hopeful spirit.

There were no real grounds for optimism, however. Despite the abundance of food and land in California, little was made available to the new arrivals. The huge farming industry took its pick of farm workers, then paid them as little as possible for long hours of work. The accommodation provided was primitive and insanitary. For the people who did not find work, the situation was

Opposite A migrant worker and his family. 'They were not farm men any more, but migrant men. And the thought, the planning, the long staring silence that had gone out to the fields, were now to the roads, to the distance, to the West.' (The Grapes of Wrath)

Machinery buried by sand during the wind storms of the 1930s in the Great Plains of the USA. The storms tore the topsoil off the farmland, creating a Dust Bowl that looked like a desert.

A breadline in New York City during the Depression. All over the USA, hungry people – women, children and men – waited every day in long queues for food and drink from relief kitchens.

even worse. Many of them had to live in a 'Hooverville', and were constantly at risk of disease and starvation. The luckiest migrants found a place in one of the federal camps, which had running water and toilets, and allowed people to maintain a sense of dignity. In *The Grapes of Wrath*, the Weedpatch federal camp is the only place where the Joads can enjoy some measure of comfort.

The Depression and the Dust Bowl brought about

lasting changes in American life. While the big growers 'farmed on paper', explains Steinbeck, the migrants 'changed their social life – changed as in the whole universe only man can change. They were not farm men any more, but migrant men.' Their connection with the land was replaced by an uneasy connection with a new industrial way of life. In *The Grapes of Wrath*, this new connection is experienced by the Joads in their enforced

reliance on an old and battered car. As they prepare to travel to California:

> The house was dead, and the fields were dead; but this truck was the active thing, the living principle. The ancient Hudson, with bent and scarred radiator screen, with grease in dusty globules at the worn edges of every moving part, with hub caps gone and caps of red dust in their places – this was the new hearth, the living centre of the family . . .

Reporting on war

The Second World War may have brought an end to the Depression, but it also brought a different kind of suffering. Nonetheless, many Americans believed they ought to take part in the fight against Fascism in Europe. Steinbeck was one of these people. He hoped for an assignment in intelligence work, but was disappointed. Since he was nearly 40 and also had a back problem, he was not an ideal candidate for the military services.

Opposite *Migrant fruit pickers in California, 1937. 'Why, I seen han'bills how they need folks to pick fruit, an' good wages,' Wilson tells Pa in* The Grapes of Wrath. *But in fact, fruit picking paid barely enough to survive and was back-breaking work.*

American soldiers making friends with local children in Britain during the Second World War. John Steinbeck visited Britain while working in Europe as a war correspondent.

31

John Steinbeck and his friend Max Wagner in London. They are surrounded by the rubble left by bombs from German planes during the Second World War.

His literary contributions to the war were welcomed, however. In 1942 he wrote *The Moon is Down*, a story about the Nazi occupation of Norway and the evils of Fascism, and *Bombs Away: The Story of a Bomber Team*, which was meant to encourage recruitment to the Army Air Corps. He also went to Hollywood to help in the production of films that would boost American morale. He wrote the

screenplay for *Lifeboat*, a glorification of the merchant marines that was produced by Alfred Hitchcock in 1944.

Steinbeck did finally get to the front lines of the war. He went to Europe and North Africa as a war correspondent for the New York *Herald Tribune*. He was appalled by much of what he saw, especially by the fighting on the beachhead at Salerno. 'There is no dignity in death in battle,' he

American troops filing aboard transport ships on their way to a surprise landing behind German lines. Steinbeck was horrified by the sight of the death and suffering caused by war.

observed much later in *East of Eden*. 'Mostly that is a splashing about of human meat and fluid, and the result is filthy.' When he returned to the USA, he was emotionally depressed by his experience of war. He was also physically weakened by it. Both his eardrums had been burst by the deafening sound of battle in Italy, so that he suffered occasional blackouts and loss of memory. He had also twisted an ankle while jumping out of a landing craft during the invasion.

Steinbeck was again confronted with war in the 1960s, when the USA became involved in the Vietnam conflict.

Initially, he saw the war as a fight for human dignity and individual freedom. He was so sure about this position that he reassured President Lyndon Johnson about the moral rightness of American intervention. 'To many of [Steinbeck's] friends and intimates,' writes a biographer, 'this attitude seemed a change of heart and an abandonment of everything he had stood for.'

Steinbeck decided in the mid 1960s to see for himself what was going on in Vietnam. At the age of 65, he went there as a correspondent for *Newsday*, with his wife, Elaine. In his usual determined manner, he went on dangerous

Steinbeck (on the right) in Vietnam during the Vietnam War. While working as a war correspondent, he went out 'in the really hairy boondocks, in the waist-deep paddies where your boots suck in mud that holds like glue.'

combat missions in the jungle. He enjoyed the company of the American soldiers, relishing as always the military spirit. 'Yesterday,' he said in one of his letters, 'I was out with a really good bunch of men. We climbed out of

ditches, went through houses, questioned people. . .'

But the more that Steinbeck saw in Vietnam, the more he doubted the value of the presence of American troops. After his return to the USA, he despaired that, 'We seem

to be sinking deeper and deeper into the mire . . . I am pretty sure by now that the people running the war have neither conception nor control of it.'

Steinbeck and politics

Many people who have heard of Steinbeck but not read his fiction think of him as an extreme left-winger. This is not surprising, given his choice of subject matter and his reputation. Steinbeck was frequently denounced as a 'dangerous Communist' after the publication of *The Grapes of Wrath*. He was seen as a troublemaker and there were frequent threats on his life and property. A friendly sheriff warned him against staying in a hotel. 'The boys got a rape case set up for you,' he explained. 'A dame will come in, tear off her clothes, scratch her face and scream and you try to talk yourself out of that one. They won't touch your book but there's easier ways.'

But in fact, as a recent biographer has claimed, 'It would be a mistake to think . . . [of Steinbeck] as a political radical'. He was more of a 'New Deal' Democrat with strong ideas of right and wrong, and a deep respect for the rights of the individual. He was not inciting his readers to tear apart the basis of American society. Rather, he was urging those

Opposite *American soldiers on patrol in the jungle of Vietnam. At first Steinbeck supported American involvement in Vietnam, but his visit convinced him that it was a mistake.*

The arrest of a Communist organizer during a demonstration in New York against high rents. It was widely – and mistakenly – claimed that Steinbeck was a Communist.

in power to improve conditions *before* the poor became desperate enough to 'take by force what they need'. Steinbeck believed that 'the line between hunger and

Soldiers in the National Guard protecting a mill in 1934. It was not unusual in the years of the Depression for soldiers to guard factories and mills against striking workers.

anger is a thin line,' and that in California this line was being crossed. 'California is not very far from civil war,' he observed, adding, 'I hope it can be averted.'

In Dubious Battle is a novel about a disastrous fruit-pickers' strike. It is often thought to be Steinbeck's most radical work, because of its focus on Communist organizers. But in fact, Steinbeck was opposed to the idea of Communism. 'Now mark my prophecy,' he once remarked. 'The so-called Communist system will break up and destroy itself in horrible civil wars because it is not a permanent workable system. It will fly apart from its own flaws.' In any case, we are shown in *In Dubious Battle* that the battle of the Communist organizers is dubious indeed. There is little to choose between them and the landowners.

The struggle for justice

Steinbeck may not have sided with the political left or the political right, but he did have strong views on social justice. Like Tom Joad in *The Grapes of Wrath*, he was 'completely partisan on the idea of working people to the end that they may eat what they raise, wear what they weave, use what they produce, and share in the work of their hands and heads.' He firmly defended every person's right to a dignified existence and condemned anyone – Communist or capitalist – who interfered with this right. He himself did what he could to help the downtrodden of society. He wrote to his literary agent that:

> The death of children by starvation in our valleys is simply staggering . . . If I can sell the articles I'll use the proceeds for serum and such. Codliver oil would give the live kids a better chance. Of course no individual effort will help. Ten thousand people are affected in one area. Anyway, I'll do what I can.

Opposite *The entrance for so-called 'colored' people at a cinema in Florida in the 1930s. This separation of blacks from whites, which appalled Steinbeck, was called Jim Crow. It was common in the USA until the 1960s.*

Steinbeck's most powerful contribution to the struggle for justice, however, was made by his pen. In *Of Mice and Men*, the impossibility of Lennie's dream 'to live off the fatta the lan' ' underlines the vulnerability of the landless poor. It also demonstrates the moral failure of American society, which has no place for a simple man like Lennie. In *The Pearl*, the dreams of the poor are shown to be equally hopeless. The inequities of Mexican society are so deep that Kino and Juana have no chance of building a better life. When they try to sell their valuable pearl for a fair price, they provoke the anger of the powerful and the death of their son. As Kino's brother tells him, 'You have

SAENGER
Colored
Entrance

ADMISSION
10¢

SAENGER
· COLORED ENTRANCE ·

NOW PLAYING

OUT WEST WITH
THE HARDYS

STONE
Mickey
ROONEY
Cecilia
PARKER
Fay
HOLDEN

INSURANCE

An unemployed man tries to earn a living by selling apples outside his Hooverville home.

defied . . . the whole structure, the whole way of life.' In *The Grapes of Wrath*, Steinbeck himself took a defiant position. He exposed the wretched conditions of the American landless poor and – as we shall see in the following section of this book – gave a powerful voice to their suffering.

2 *The Grapes of Wrath*

The Grapes of Wrath is the straightforward story of three generations of the Joad family, who are forced off their Oklahoma farm during the Depression. They join a stream of dispossessed farmers heading down Highway 66, the road that leads to California and a new life. They travel in discomfort in an old car converted into a truck, and the grandparents die on the way. Conditions get even worse

A map showing the states of the USA.

Boys playing at a camp for migrant families. Like Ruthie and Winfield in The Grapes of Wrath, *these children had to try to earn money and could not go to school.*

when they arrive in California. There are too few jobs available, which in any case are badly paid. The Joads are lucky to get a place for a while in a primitive but clean government camp. By the end of the novel, the family is breaking up and has no reasonable prospect of work, food or shelter. This suffering was endured by nearly all the so-called 'Okies' (people from Oklahoma) and other landless people who migrated to California in the 1930s. But it was unknown to most people until *The Grapes of Wrath* took the American public by storm in 1939.

In 1936, Steinbeck wrote a series of newspaper articles about the conditions of migrant workers in California. He then thought of putting this information together in the form of a novel. After a couple of unsatisfactory beginnings, he settled down in 1938 to write *The Grapes of Wrath* and finished it within five months.

He was determined to paint an accurate picture of the migrants' experience. 'I'm trying to write history while it's happening and I don't want to be wrong,' he explained. Joining a group of families moving west from Oklahoma,

he was able to observe the conditions in which they travelled and the difficulties they met on their arrival in California. A most valuable source of information was Tom Collins, who administered the Weedpatch Government Sanitary Camp that features in the novel. Steinbeck watched Collins at work in the camp and mingled with the people living there. He was impressed by the democratic organization of the camp, which was governed by a committee elected from the people. He honoured Collins's achievement by dedicating *The Grapes* not only to his wife, but also 'To Tom, who lived it.'

The source of the title

The title of *The Grapes of Wrath* is taken from the first verse of *The Battle Hymn of the Republic* – 'He is trampling out the vintage where the grapes of wrath are stored.' The *Hymn* was written during the American Civil War to boost the morale of Union soldiers fighting to 'make men free' by ending slavery in the South. Steinbeck thought that the righteous spirit of the *Hymn* was fitting for a novel about injustice and suffering. He asked his editor to publish the lyrics at the end of the book – '*all all all* the verses of the Battle Hymn. They're all pertinent and they're all exciting.'

A scene from the film version of The Grapes of Wrath. *Steinbeck described the film as 'a hard, straight picture in which the actors are submerged so completely that it looks and feels like a documentary film and certainly it has a hard, truthful ring.' Tom Joad (on the left) is played by Henry Fonda.*

The reference in the title to 'grapes' is especially appropriate because many of the migrants sought work in the Californian vineyards. Steinbeck's 'grapes of wrath' refer in particular to the threat of a harvest of violence, grown from seeds of anger that had been sown by the landowners' greed. 'In the eyes of the hungry,' he warns in the novel, 'there is a growing wrath. In the souls of the people the grapes of wrath are filling and growing heavy, growing heavy for the vintage.'

Educating the reader
Steinbeck did not write *The Grapes of Wrath* to entertain his readers. 'I'm not writing a satisfying story,' he told his

A family from Kansas arrives at a camp. Most migrants sold their animals to buy a car, but this family has kept its mules.

editor when he had finished the novel. 'I've done my damndest to rip a reader's nerves to rags, I don't want him satisfied.' *The Grapes of Wrath* is a didactic novel, in the sense that Steinbeck wanted to educate his readers. He explained when he was working on *East of Eden* that:

> there is one purpose in writing that I can see, beyond simply doing it interestingly. It is the duty of the writer to lift up, to extend, to encourage. If the written word has contributed anything at all to our developing species and our half developed culture, it is this: Great writing has been a staff to lean on, a mother to consult, a wisdom to pick up stumbling folly, a strength in weakness and a courage to support sick cowardice.

Didactic fiction is not fashionable today. But in the eighteenth and nineteenth centuries it was common for novelists to write with the purpose of 'teaching' their readers. *Great Expectations* by the Englishman Charles Dickens, and *Huckleberry Finn* by the American Mark Twain, are two nineteenth-century classics that are didactic.

But of course, a novel is not going to be successful just

The Joads get ready to leave Oklahoma in their overloaded jalopy. In this scene from the film of The Grapes of Wrath, *Ma (bottom left) shows her anxiety about the long journey to California.*

because it says something important. It also needs to be written well, so that the reader is drawn into the story. Any careful reading of a novel, therefore, must take into consideration not only *what* an author wrote, but also *how* she or he wrote. To understand *The Grapes of Wrath*, we must look not only at the story of the Joads, but also at the narrative techniques that Steinbeck used to tell the story and to convey the social message it contains.

The structure of Steinbeck's novels

The structure of a novel contributes to its overall effect. *Of Mice and Men* has some of the impact of drama, for example, because Steinbeck planned it as a play even while he was writing it as a novel. Each of the six chapters is confined to one scene, which is carefully described, and characters come into the scene and go off again. As the director of the first dramatic production of the story told Steinbeck, 'It drops almost naturally into play form and no one knows that better than you.'

Steinbeck thought carefully about the structure of *The Grapes*. 'I've been on this design and balance for a long time,' he said, 'and I think I know how I want it . . . The balance is there.' The novel divides cleanly into three sections. First, there is the section about the Joads in Oklahoma, then a section about the Joads on the road, and finally a section about the Joads in California. Running through these three sections are short chapters narrated by the author. This step-by step structure of *The Grapes* underlines the idea of the journey in the story. It also creates a simplicity that helps the reader to grasp the novel's meaning.

Intervention by the narrator

Some novelists write in such a way that we, the readers, are not made aware of their role as creator of the story. Others intervene with comments and opinions of their own. Steinbeck appears to have admired novels where the narrator was invisible. In *Cannery Row*, he remarks that:

> When you collect marine animals there are certain flat worms so delicate that they are almost impossible to capture whole, for they break and tatter under the touch. You must let them ooze and crawl of their own will on to a knife blade and then lift them gently into your bottle of sea water. *And perhaps that might be the way to write this book – to open the page and to let the stories crawl in by themselves.* [emphasis added]

In *Cannery Row* and *In Dubious Battle*, Steinbeck goes a long way towards achieving this effect.

But in most of his novels, he seems to hover in the background. Even in *Of Mice and Men*, where the dramatic structure removes the need for authorial comment, he

Opposite *This farmer from South Dakota is on his way, he hopes, to a better life in Oregon. He is one of the 'people in flight, refugees from dust and shrinking land, from the . . . desert's slow northward invasion.'* (The Grapes of Wrath)

offers his own perspective on events. His description of Curley's wife after death, for instance, reveals his sympathy for her: 'The meanness and the plannings and the discontent and the ache for attention were all gone from her face. She was very pretty and simple, and her face was sweet and young.'

A deserted town in Oklahoma, 1938. The effects of the Dust Bowl forced many people to go in search of work.

In *The Grapes*, there is a great deal of authorial comment. The novel is interspersed with 16 interchapters (sometimes called 'intercalary' chapters), in none of which do any characters – even the Joads – appear in any significant fashion. Instead, Steinbeck speaks directly to the reader, enlarging on the difficulties that beset the Joads

and adding any information that seemed to him important. In this way, he made sure that his readers would understand fully the social context of the story he was telling. Such a device may or may not enhance the artistic merit of *The Grapes of Wrath*. But it certainly helped Steinbeck to convey his message.

Portrayal of character

It would be more effective, said Steinbeck, to focus on one family in *The Grapes* than to write more generally about the suffering of the landless poor. 'It means very little to know that a million Chinese are starving,' he pointed out, 'unless you know one Chinese who is starving.' Some critics have complained, however, that it is difficult to develop any sense of 'knowing' Steinbeck's characters. Few of them

In this scene from the film of The Grapes of Wrath, *the Joads eat together before they start their journey. Despite the lack of any luxuries, this meal in a real house is much more comfortable than the meals they will have on the road.*

display the complex mixture of different human emotions that we find in most people. In *The Grapes*, for example, the poor and the suffering are well-intentioned and good. The rich and powerful and their allies (like the vigilantes and police), on the other hand, are brutal and mean. In his prologue to *The Pearl*, Steinbeck commented that, 'as with all retold tales that are in people's hearts, there are only good and bad things and black and white things and good

and evil things and no in-between anywhere.' This seems to have been true of the tales in Steinbeck's heart, at least in the case of *The Grapes*.

Images and symbols

Steinbeck was preoccupied with nature and biology and took many of his images and symbols from the natural world. In *Of Mice and Men*, we are told in the first few pages that, 'Lennie dabbled his big paw in the water,' and Lennie is likened on different occasions to a dog, a bear and a coyote. When things go badly for Kino in *The Pearl*, his limbs stir 'like those of a crushed bug.' In *The Grapes*, 'the cars of the migrant people crawled out like bugs.' By likening his victims of society to animals and insects, Steinbeck highlights their vulnerability. He also creates a contrast between the world of nature and modern industrial society.

Many critics have identified the turtle in the early chapters of *The Grapes* as the major symbol of the novel. The turtle and the Joad family are both travelling west. They are both determined to keep going, because they don't know what else to do. 'Joad,' writes Steinbeck, 'plodded along, dragging his cloud of dust behind him. A little bit ahead he saw the high-domed shell of a land turtle, crawling slowly along through the dust, its legs working stiffly and jerkily.' Both the Joads and the turtle are victims of gratuitous cruelty, which in the turtle's case is epitomized by a truck driver's deliberate swerve to kill it.

Images from the Bible run through the novel. The exodus of the Joads from Oklahoma to California is like the exodus of the Israelites from the misery of Egypt into Canaan. Like the Israelites, the Joads hope to find paradise, but instead find hostility. At the end of *The Grapes*, there is a stable scene that recalls the birth of Jesus. But Steinbeck's image of 'madonna and child' is strikingly different – Rosasharn is not feeding her baby, who was born dead, but a starving man she has never met before. She is following the teaching of Jim Casy, the preacher of the gospel of social justice, who has the same initials as Jesus Christ.

Use of language

Steinbeck was keenly aware of the power of language. While writing *East of Eden*, he warned himself, 'Oh! but

Opposite *'The houses were left vacant on the land, and the land was vacant because of this . . . The doors of the empty houses swung open, and drifted back and forth in the wind.'* (The Grapes of Wrath)

watch for terseness. Don't let it ever be adjectivally descriptive. I must hold description to an absolute minimum.' Elsewhere he mentions his wish that 'the words be very clear and sharp like good knives.' He seems to have been aiming for the clarity and precision that was achieved by Ernest Hemingway, another American novelist of the time.

But Steinbeck did not have the narrative gifts of a writer like Hemingway. His hard work sometimes produced inappropriate and ineffective language. For example, the choice of verbs in the sentence, 'The houses belched people; the doorways spewed out children,' adds nothing to *The Pearl* but clumsy overstatement. In *The Grapes*, the characters are supposed to speak just like the people they are based on. But instead, their speech seems artificial and repetitive. One critic complains that Ma is always saying, 'We'll figger somepin out.' Even worse, he says, is the fact that Steinbeck allows 'his Joads for six hundred pages to figger and innerduce and understan', to git a-sayin' and go a-billygoatin'.' It does seem that he had difficulty in producing language that was authentic.

Opposite *Ernest Hemingway, an American novelist who won the Nobel Prize for Literature in 1954. After Hemingway's suicide in 1961, Steinbeck remarked that 'he has had the most profound effect on writing – more than anyone I can think of.'*

Sentence structure

Steinbeck used the form of his sentences and paragraphs to enhance their meaning. The accounts of the journeys taken by the turtle and the Joads, for example, are constructed in such a way as to convey a sense of the travellers' effort and exhaustion. The turtle's climb up the embankment is described in an extremely long paragraph, which gives the reader a feel of the length and difficulty of his trip. The description of Highway 66, the road that had to be taken by the Joads in order to reach California, achieves the same effect. It contains very long sentences that are made up of short phrases joined by hyphens and commas:

> 66 – the long concrete path across the country, waving gently up and down on the map, from Mississippi to Bakersfield – over the red lands and the grey lands, twisting up into the mountains, crossing the Divide and down into the bright and terrible desert, and across the desert to the mountains again, and into the rich California valleys.

Many passages in *The Grapes*, especially in the interchapters, are redolent of the Bible. If one were to read them aloud, following the punctuation, they would probably sound like the Old Testament. Steinbeck organized this effect by using 'And ' to start a number of consecutive sentences, which are made up of many short phrases. This method of referring to the Bible, together with the novel's biblical images, attaches a kind of moral

Granma lies dead in the film of The Grapes of Wrath. *By the time the Joads reach California, the family unit has been broken by death and sorrow. 'We're crackin' up,' says Ma to Tom. 'There ain't no fambly now.'*

authority to Steinbeck's protest against the suffering of the poor.

The novel's ending
Throughout the novel, Rosasharn is pregnant. By its end, she has given birth to a dead baby. She then uses the milk in her breasts to rescue the life of a hungry stranger, another victim of the Depression. Steinbeck's editor

A scene from the film of The Grapes of Wrath. *'The great companies did not know that the line between hunger and anger is a thin line . . . And the anger began to ferment.'*

thought this ending would shock the public and asked him to change it. Steinbeck refused. He explained that:

> It is casual – there is no fruity climax, it is not more important than any other part of the book – if there is a symbol, it is a survival symbol not a love symbol, it must be an accident, it must be a stranger, and it must be quick. To build this stranger into the structure of the book would be to warp the whole meaning of the book. The fact that

the Joads don't know him, don't care about him, have no ties to him – that is the emphasis. The giving of the breast has no more sentiment than the giving of a piece of bread.

A variety of judgements has been offered on this ending. One view is that the story tells of the gradual deterioration of the Joad family, which culminates in Rosasharn's tasteless offering of her breast. The Joads 'start off as a cheerful group full of hope and willpower,' remarks one critic, adding that by the end of the novel, they 'are spiritually bankrupt'.

A poor couple in Alabama, 1935. Small farmers who stayed on the land during the Depression suffered terrible poverty and hardship.

Most interpretations of the novel's ending are more optimistic. They suggest that the Joads are forced by their suffering to see themselves as part of a larger community. Initially they are only concerned with their own survival, but gradually they develop a sense of solidarity with other poor people. In this context, Rosasharn's gift to a stranger of 'the milk of human kindness' is a powerful symbol of togetherness and co-operation. 'When they're all workin' together, not one fella for another fella,' observes the preacher Casy, 'but one fella kind of harnessed to the whole shebang – that's right, that's holy.' This is a 'holiness' that is reserved for the landless poor, suggests Steinbeck. 'The quality of owning,' he tells the landowners, 'freezes you for ever into "I" and cuts you off for ever from the "we".'

In this scene from the film of The Grapes of Wrath, *the police are trying – without success – to provoke a riot at a dance in the Weedpatch government camp. 'If they can git a fight goin', then they can run in the cops an' say we ain't orderly. They tried it before – other places.'*

Steinbeck delivering a speech of thanks for the Nobel Prize in 1962. Before the ceremony, he told a friend that, 'I haven't an idea of what to say . . . The idea of having to stand up there and speak just scares me to death.'

Reactions to the novel

The publication of *The Grapes of Wrath* in 1939 provoked anger and criticism from the landowners. 'The Associated Farmers,' wrote Steinbeck at the time, 'keep up a steady stream of accusation that I am first a liar and second a Communist. Their vilification has a quality of hysteria

too.' The big growers claimed that Steinbeck had fabricated most of his details. They even campaigned to have the novel banned from schools and public libraries (it is still banned in some American schools and public libraries) and had the book publicly burned in Salinas on several occasions. Steinbeck was persuaded by his friends to take this anger seriously. He wrote a letter at this time saying that:

> They can't shoot me now because it would be too obvious and because I have placed certain informations in the hands of J. Edgar Hoover in case I take a nose dive. So I think I am personally safe enough except for automobile accidents etc. and rape and stuff like that so I am a little careful not to go anywhere alone nor to do anything without witnesses.

Despite the bitter attacks on *The Grapes*, it was welcomed by the American reading public. It was the top bestseller in the USA in the year of its publication and it is still, half a century later, one of the most popular American novels of all time. Dorothy Parker, the well-known short story writer and critic, called it 'the greatest American novel I have ever read.' It brought Steinbeck the Pulitzer Prize in 1940, and it was chiefly because of *The Grapes of Wrath* that he was awarded the Nobel Prize for Literature in 1962.

3 Steinbeck the Writer

Twentieth-century fiction
The horror of the First World War led many people to challenge the traditional values and culture that had dominated Europe and the USA. To many artists, there now seemed to be no real possibility of order in society and art. The painter Picasso, the musician Stravinsky, and the novelists Joyce and Proust, for example, experimented with their subject matter and tried out different kinds of form. This development in art came to be known as 'modernism'.

In the USA, modernist art reflected American concerns and issues. The novelist Sinclair Lewis satirized the 'American Dream', the belief that any hardworking individual can obtain success, wealth and happiness, in *Main Street* (1920) and *Babbit* (1922). The same sense of disillusionment can be seen in the fiction of F. Scott Fitzgerald, who shows youth's dreams turning to despair in *The Great Gatsby* (1925).

The modernist idea influenced not only the content of fiction, but also its form. The novelist Ernest Hemingway aimed for a new simplicity of expression by cutting out unnecessary words and avoiding complex sentences. This is achieved to considerable effect in *The Sun Also Rises* (1926), *A Farewell to Arms* (1929), and *For Whom the Bell Tolls* (1940). William Faulkner, a novelist who wrote about the Deep South, was more ambitious. In his effort to portray Southern society as decayed and grotesque, he jumbled up the time sequences in his novels and presented the

F. Scott Fitzgerald (1896–1940), an American novelist of the modernist period.

thoughts of his characters as rambling and uncontrolled. In this way, he used the form of his fiction to reflect its content. His best known novels are *The Sound and the Fury* (1929) and *Light in August* (1932).

Billie Holiday (1915–59), an American jazz singer who was a contemporary of Steinbeck. She was famous for her blues sound and the depth of feeling in her voice.

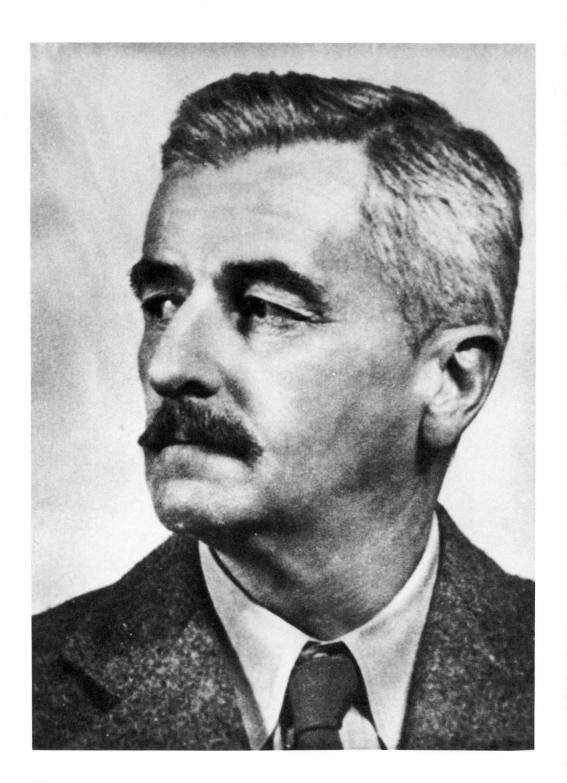

Steinbeck claimed to have little respect for some of his fellow writers. He referred with contempt to '. . . the ridiculous preoccupations of my great contemporaries, and I mean Faulkner and Hemingway, with their own immortality. It is almost as though they were fighting for billing on a tombstone.' Unlike them, Steinbeck did not attempt any innovative experiments in the form of his novels. The step-by-step construction of *The Grapes of Wrath* has none of the splintered and complex structure of novels like Faulkner's *The Sound and the Fury*. The techniques used by Steinbeck are more reminiscent of nineteenth-century 'realist' novels, in which the fictional world is made to look just like the real world.

In terms of his subject matter, however, Steinbeck showed himself to be as much a modernist as any other artist. As the twentieth century progressed, an increasing number of American writers expressed their loss of confidence in the fabric of society. In the South, Erskine Caldwell took a hard look at poor Southern life in *Tobacco Road* (1932) and *God's Little Acre* (1933). In the Mid-West, James T. Farrell portrayed slum life in Chicago in *The Studs Lonigan Trilogy* (1932–5). In *Native Son* (1940), Richard Wright presented a new black hero whose life and acts convey the power of the racism in American society. The hero of Ralph Ellison's *Invisible Man* (1952) discovers that because of his black skin, he is 'invisible' to American whites. John Steinbeck was by no means alone, then, in giving a powerful and critical voice to the oppressed and deprived members of American society.

The influence of *Morte d'Arthur*
Steinbeck's parents and relatives were anxious for him to enjoy literature. In his earliest years, he rebelled against their encouragement. He remembered when he was an adult that:

> . . . words – written or printed – were devils, and books, because they gave me pain, were my enemies . . . Literature was in the air around me. The Bible I absorbed through my skin. My uncles exuded Shakespeare, and *Pilgrim's Progress* was mixed with my mother's milk. But these things came into my ears. They were sounds, rhythms, figures. Books were printed demons – the tongs and thumbscrews of outrageous persecution.

Opposite *William Faulkner (1897–1962), an innovative American novelist who received the Nobel Prize in 1949. 'Sure he's a good writer,' wrote Steinbeck of Faulkner, 'but he's turning into a god-damned phoney.'*

All these resentments vanished when he was introduced by an aunt to Sir Thomas Malory's *Morte d'Arthur*, a prose version of the Arthurian legends. It was written in the fifteenth century by Sir Thomas while he was in prison. At first, said Steinbeck later, he 'stared at the black print with hatred.' But gradually. . .

. . . the pages opened and let me in. The magic happened. The Bible and Shakespeare and *Pilgrim's Progress* belonged to everyone. But this was mine – it was a cut version of the Caxton *Morte d'Arthur* of Thomas Malory. I loved the old spelling of the words – and the words no longer used. Perhaps a passionate love of the English language opened to me from this one book.

These stories about the chivalry, love and religious zeal of Arthur and the Knights of the Round Table had a fascination for John. He loved their language, mystery and sense of gallantry.

An illustration for the prose romance Morte d'Arthur, *which was written in the fifteenth century by Thomas Malory. It introduced Steinbeck to the joys of reading and shaped his decision to become a writer.*

Steinbeck was later to describe *Morte d'Arthur* as the force that shaped his decision to be a writer. The influence of the book on his fiction can be seen in many ways. In *Tortilla Flat* (1935), for example, the poor and illiterate Mexican peasants in California are described in terms of the Knights of King Arthur's Round Table. A biographer has observed that John 'really did believe, with his whole heart, in Lancelot, and the Knight's nobility became for him both a model and a measure of the love, generosity, loyalty, and sense of duty that a man may bring to life.'

After his exposure to Malory, Steinbeck read widely and with enjoyment. From the family library, he chose works by Milton, Dostoevsky, Flaubert, George Eliot and Thomas Hardy. He also read Shakespeare and was familiar with the King James Bible. The titles of his novels indicate the breadth of his reading. *In Dubious Battle*, for example, is a phrase from Milton's *Paradise Lost*, and *The Winter of our Discontent* is taken from the first scene of Shakespeare's *Richard III*. The title *Of Mice and Men* comes from the poem *To A Mouse*, by the eighteenth-century Scottish poet, Robert Burns. Literary references like these do not betray a pretentious intellect. Rather, they reveal Steinbeck's pleasure in the world of books.

Becoming a writer
From his earliest years, recalls his sister Esther, 'John always had to write things.' He was usually short of money, so he wrote poems as presents on family birthdays. As a child, he said later, he 'used to sit in that little room upstairs . . . and write little stories and little pieces and send them out to magazines under a false name and I never knew what happened to them because I never put a return address on them.'

Steinbeck loved the feeling of using words to build something that had a meaning of its own. In the dedication he wrote for *East of Eden*, he refers to 'the indescribable job of creation.' In *Cannery Row*, he remarks that, 'The word is a symbol and a delight which sucks up men and scenes, trees, plants, factories, and Pekinese. Then the Thing becomes the Word and back to Thing again, but warped and woven into a fantastic pattern.' It seemed to him that there was some really useful purpose in being a writer. In his speech of thanks for the Nobel Prize, he referred to his 'pride in my profession and in the great and good men

Opposite *Esther Steinbeck, one of John Steinbeck's three sisters.*

who have practised it through the ages . . . Literature is as old as speech. It grew out of human need for it, and it has not changed except to become more needed.'

He was never a confident writer, though. After sending *Of Mice and Men* to a publisher, he wrote that he had 'of course heard nothing from it. I don't know whether it is any good or not.' He was not even sure, he said, that he *wanted* to be famous. 'I am scared to death of popularity,' he admitted, because 'it has ruined everyone I know.' At no time did he develop false illusions about himself because he was famous. The fact that he was a bestselling novelist, he pointed out, did not mean he understood the world better than anyone else:

I, as a novelist, am a product not only of my own time but of all the flags and tatters, the myth and prejudice, the faith and filth that preceded me . . . A novelist is a kind of flypaper to which everything adheres. His job then is to reassemble life into some kind of order.

Steinbeck's fiction

Steinbeck's first published novel, *Cup of Gold* (1929), a historical adventure story about a famous pirate, was not successful. His next two novels, *The Pastures of Heaven* (1932) and *To A God Unknown* (1933), were set in California and were better received. He finally achieved a bestseller with *Tortilla Flat* (1935), tales about poor drifters in Monterey. It was followed in 1936 by the controversial *In Dubious Battle*.

Of Mice and Men was highly praised when it was published as a novel in 1937. It was also a smash hit on Broadway, running for 207 performances. The publication of *The Red Pony* in three parts in 1937 was also popular, as was *The Long Valley* the year after. In 1939, *The Grapes of Wrath* established Steinbeck as a major novelist to be ranked with writers like Hemingway and Faulkner.

During the Second World War, Steinbeck wrote the patriotic *Bombs Away* and *The Moon is Down*, which have been judged as worse than second-rate by many critics. In 1945, 'The Pearl of the World' (it was called *The Pearl* when it was published in book form in 1947) was printed in a women's magazine and was warmly received. The same year saw the publication of *Cannery Row*, a portrayal of the women and men living on the edge of society in the Cannery Row area of Monterey. It was called a 'very

Opposite *John and Elaine Steinbeck with John's two sons from his marriage to Gwyn – John IV [far left] and Thom.*

Allied soldiers in Norway fighting the Germans during the Second World War. Steinbeck's novel, The Moon is Down, *is about the reaction of a Norwegian town to German occupation.*

poisoned cream-puff' because of its matter-of-fact references to sex and prostitutes. In 1947, *The Wayward Bus* was published and chosen as a Book-of-the-Month Club selection.

Steinbeck became less successful as a writer as he grew older. *Burning Bright* (1950), failed both as a novel and as a play. The major creative production of Steinbeck's later years was *East of Eden* (1952), a saga set in the Salinas valley of his childhood. 'This is my big book,' he said, 'and it has to be a big book, and because it is new in form although old in pace it has to be excellent in every detail.' The novel was popular, especially when it was made into a film starring James Dean, the American heart-throb of the fifties. But critics agree that it does not achieve the literary merit of some earlier works. They are more enthusiastic about the collection of letters Steinbeck wrote to his editor while working on the novel. *This Journal of a Novel: The East of Eden Letters* (1969), is an ongoing commentary on the progress of the novel, which allows the reader to understand something about the craft of writing fiction.

Steinbeck's last – and not very successful – novels were *Sweet Thursday* (1954), *The Short Reign of Pippin IV* (1957) and *The Winter of Our Discontent* (1960). They show that he retained his keen interest in ordinary men and women until the end of his life. This interest motivated *Travels with Charley in Search of America* (1962), an account of a trip through America with his dog, Charley. 'The people I want to listen to,' he said before going on the trip, 'are . . . the man in a field who isn't likely to know my name even if he heard it.'

Opposite James Dean, the American heart-throb who acted in the film of Steinbeck's East of Eden *(1955). He also starred in* Rebel Without a Cause *(1955) and was seen as a symbol of rebellion against middle-class values. He was killed in a car crash in 1955.*

Steinbeck and film

It is a sign of Steinbeck's appeal to the general public that he had more success with cinema than any other serious American writer. His creative imagination produced thirteen films – some were based upon his novels and some were written by him as screenplays. *Viva Zapata!* (1952), for example, was an original screenplay by Steinbeck about Emiliano Zapata and the Mexican Revolution. Altogether, Steinbeck's involvement in cinema produced 25 Academy Award nominations, including three for him as best screenwriter of the year. Some of the films, such as *The Grapes of Wrath* and *East of Eden*, are considered classics.

John Steinbeck and Charley, his poodle. In 1960 they travelled in a truck through the USA, so that Steinbeck could talk to people from all walks of life. He wrote about the trip in Travels with Charley in Search of America.

Opposite *John Wayne and Kirk Douglas in a Western. The film of* The Grapes of Wrath *differed from films like this, by making a serious effort to portray the social problems of the time.*

The Grapes has a special place in the history of cinema because it went beyond mere entertainment to bring 'as close as any film in Hollywood's prolific turnout to exposing the contradictions and inequities at the heart of American life.' Steinbeck was so keen that the film remain faithful to the real situation, as it is depicted in the novel,

that he arranged for Tom Collins, the administrator of the Weedpatch migrant camp, to be the technical director of the film. John Ford, the producer, shared his concern and handled the film as if it were a documentary. As a result, said the folksinger Woody Guthrie, the film 'had more thinkin' in it than 99 per cent of the celluloid that we're tangled up in in the moving pictures today.' He urged the readers of a workingmen's newspaper to see the film:

> Go to see 'Grapes of Wrath', pardner, go to see it and don't miss. You was the star in that picture. Go and see your own self, and your own words and your own songs.

'What actually is' and 'what should be'

The careful presentation of reality in the novel and film of *The Grapes of Wrath* is characteristic of most of Steinbeck's work. His keen sensitivity to the truth of any situation was both the cause and the product of an interest in 'nonteleological' thinking. He shared his interest in this method of thought with a close friend, Ed Ricketts, who – like Doc in *Cannery Row* – worked at a laboratory on Cannery Row in Monterey.

The two friends went to the Gulf of California in 1940 to study the marine life of the shorelines. The trip enabled them to develop their ideas on 'nonteleological' thought, which was based on a parallel between human existence and biological life (like that found in a tidepool). They collaborated on *The Sea of Cortez* (1941), which gives an explanation of 'nonteleological' thought:

> Nonteleological ideas derive through 'is' thinking ... [and] consider events as outgrowths and expressions rather than as results; conscious acceptance as a desideratum, and certainly as an all-important prerequisite. Nonteleological thinking concerns itself primarily not with what should be, or could be, or might be, but rather with what actually 'is' – attempting at most to answer the already sufficiently difficult questions *what* or *how*, instead of *why*.

Opposite Ed Ricketts, a close friend of Steinbeck. Together they worked out their ideas on 'nonteleological' thought, which influenced some of Steinbeck's fiction.

In other words, 'the truest reason for anything's being so is that it *is*.'

Steinbeck addressed the questions of 'what' and 'how' with meticulous care. In *Tortilla Flat* and *Cannery Row*, he offered observations on the drifters of Monterey with an accuracy that is almost scientific. These books were

conscious attempts at a 'nonteleological' view of life and art, so the question of 'why' does not arise. But in stories like *The Grapes* and *The Pearl*, which tell of the injustice suffered by the poor, Steinbeck could not limit himself to observation and description. He also raised the issue of 'what should be, or could be, or might be', because he was so aware of what should *not* be.

Steinbeck worked hard to depict social problems in accurate detail, but he also showed why they should stop. In the case of racism, for example, he describes *how* it functions and *what* kind of harm it produces – for the Mexican Indians in *The Pearl*, for American blacks in *Of Mice and Men*, and for the so-called 'Okies' in *The Grapes*. But he also shows *why* racism is not acceptable in a civilized society. In *Of Mice and Men*, he urges his reader to imagine the feelings of Crooks, who is made to live apart from the other ranch-hands merely because he is black. Crooks asks Lennie, 'S'pose you couldn't go into the

Opposite *Ed Ricketts exploring tidepools in 1948.*

A meeting of the Ku Klux Klan, a secret American society that hates Blacks, Jews and Communists. When Curley's wife tells Crooks in Of Mice and Men, *'I could get you strung up on a tree so easy it ain't even funny,' she is referring to the Klan's history of lynching black people.*

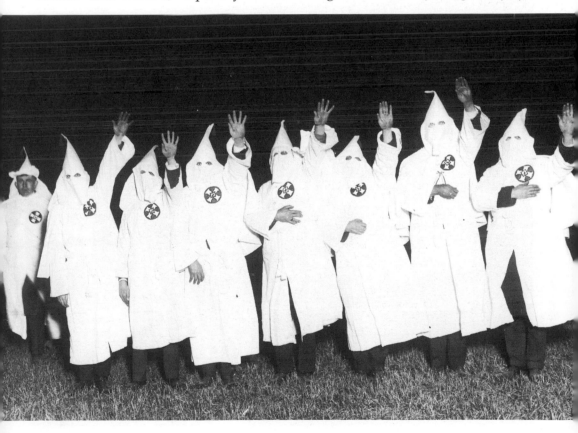

Children tying and cutting tobacco leaves. In the years of the Depression, the children of the poor had to work hard to help their families survive. In 1938, Steinbeck wrote that, 'The death of children by starvation in our valleys is simply staggering.'

bunk-house and play rummy 'cause you was black. How'd you like that?' This has the effect of making readers wonder how *they* would tolerate such treatment.

In his portrayal of women, Steinbeck shows the same sensitivity both to 'what actually is' and to 'what should [and should not] be'. In *Of Mice and Men*, the only woman in the story is not given a name. She is referred to as 'Curley's wife', which defines her solely in terms of her relationship with a man. So far, the identity she is given reflects a common perception of women in American society. It is consistent with the perception of the men on the ranch, who see Curley's wife only as a slut or a wife, not as a woman in her own right.

But a deeper reading of the story reveals Steinbeck's indignation at the treatment that Curley's wife receives from men. We are led to feel pity for her dependent position and to understand her behaviour. In a letter to an actress who was about to play the role of Curley's wife, Steinbeck indicated the source of her unhappiness:

> She is a nice, kind girl and not a floozy. No man has ever considered her as anything except a girl to try to make. She has never talked to a man except in the sexual fencing conversation. She is not highly sexed particularly but knows instinctively that if she is to be noticed at all, it will be because some one finds her sexually desirable.

It was always important for Steinbeck to describe reality as fully as possible. But this was not enough when the subject matter of his stories was poverty and injustice. He then worked hard to show his reader why it was necessary to bring about change. 'A writer who does not passionately believe in the perfectibility of man,' he thought, 'has no dedication nor any membership in literature.'

Steinbeck's reputation

Steinbeck has rarely been given full approval by literary critics. One critic describes him as 'a great artist with great flaws'. Another refers to his 'decline as a writer', saying that he failed to progress in an even manner from book to book. Yet another admires the 'human achievement' of his work but complains that he 'fell into bathos in everything he wrote.' No wonder Steinbeck described literary criticism as 'a kind of ill-tempered parlour game in which nobody gets kissed!'

Opposite *A drinking fountain for so-called 'colored' people at a streetcar terminal in Oklahoma City, 1939. In* Of Mice and Men, *Crooks explains that he is made to live apart from the white ranch hands because he is black. 'They play cards in there, but I can't play because I'm black.'*

Steinbeck's reading public, however, welcomed his fiction with uncritical enjoyment. In the half century since *The Grapes of Wrath* was first published, 14 million copies have been sold all over the world. Steinbeck may not have produced the sophisticated fiction of an intellectual writer like William Faulkner. But his novels have a meaning for ordinary people that few novelists have been able to achieve. In straightforward prose, they celebrate the sorrow and the joy of daily existence. They also give a dignity to the struggle for survival that is so often a part of human experience, especially for the poor. One woman who suffered through the Depression read *The Grapes of Wrath* many years later. 'That was like reliving my whole life,' she said. 'I was never so proud of poor people before as I was after I read this book.'

John Steinbeck, whose Grapes of Wrath *is one of the most important American novels ever written.*

Glossary

Aesthetic Concerned with the beautiful, with artistic sense and taste.

American Civil War The war between the North (the Union) and the South (the Confederacy) in the USA (1861–65). The North was fighting to end slavery in the South.

'Arkies' People from the state of Arkansas, USA.

Biography Someone's life story written by another person.

Cannery Row A row of sardine-canning factories in Monterey, California.

Communism The theory and system of the ownership of all property and wealth by the community as a whole.

Democrat In the USA, someone who supports the Democratic political party. President Roosevelt, who implemented the **New Deal**, was a Democrat.

Depression In economics, a period of falling prices and unemployment, like the Great Depression of the 1930s in the USA.

Didactic literature Literature which aims to teach the reader something.

Drama A play performed on stage by actors.

Dust Bowl A vast desert area in the Great Plains, USA, where the topsoil was eroded and then blown away by winds in the 1930s.

Fascism An extremely right-wing political system, which historically has gone to any lengths to take power. The **Nazis** were Fascists.

Federal In the USA, having to do with the central government of the nation.

Fiction A written story with characters and events that have been invented. Novels and short stories are works of fiction.

Hearth The floor of a fireplace, hence the centre of family life.

Hero/heroine The chief character in a story or play, who is usually good.

Hooverville A collection of huts, tents and broken cars that was home for the unemployed during the American Depression of the 1930s.

Intercalary Something that is added or inserted.

Intervention The interference of one person or one state in the affairs of another.

Itinerant A person who travels from place to place.

Left-winger A political label which was first applied to those who supported radical change in France in the nineteenth century. It is still used to refer to people who side with the poor and oppose those with money and power.

Liberal A nineteenth-century term to describe a set of political principles, which include a belief in the importance of individual freedom and a dislike of traditions which favour the 'establishment'.

Migrant A person who travels from one place to another.

Modernism A tendency among artists during the first three-quarters of the twentieth century to break with traditional style and to experiment with subject matter and form.

Narrative The telling of a story. Novels and short stories are narratives.

Narrator The teller of a story.

Nazi A member of the German National Socialist Party, the Fascist political party that ruled Germany under Hitler from 1933–45.

New Deal The economic principles implemented by President Franklin D. Roosevelt to rescue American people from the suffering of the 1930s Depression.

Nonteleological Relating to the idea that nature operates on an *is* basis, making the question *why* irrelevant (as explained by Steinbeck and Ed Ricketts).

Novel An invented story of book-length.

Occupation In war, the taking over of another country by armed forces.

'Okies' People from the state of Oklahoma, USA.

Parable A fable or story, told to illustrate some particular way of looking at the world.

Plot The series of connected events that holds a story together (in other words, the story-line).

Prose Language that is written as we speak it, not in lines of verse.

Realist novel A novel set in a fictional world that seems to be just like the real world.

Republican In the USA, someone who supports the Republican political party.

Saga A long and complex story, weaving together many characters and events.

Sharecropper A tenant farmer who works on the land for a share of the crop.

Teleological Relating to the theory that there is an overall design or purpose in nature.

Vietnam War The involvement of the USA in a war in Vietnam, a country in south-east Asia that had been partitioned in 1954. The Americans sent troops in the 1960s to support the government of South Vietnam against local revolutionaries and the government of the North. The troops were withdrawn in 1973.

List of Dates

1902	27 February: John Steinbeck born in Salinas, California.
1903	First aeroplane flight by Wright brothers.
1907	Washing machine invented.
1910	Mexican Revolution.
1912	*Titanic* sinks while crossing the Atlantic.
1914	Outbreak of First World War.
1915	Sinking of *Lusitania* by Germans, angering USA.
1916	Death of Henry James the novelist.
1917	USA joins Allies in First World War.
1918	First World War ends.
1919	JS graduates from High School.
1920	JS starts at Stanford University.
1925	JS drops out of university without a degree. Television invented.
1926–29	JS works as unskilled labourer while writing.
1927	First talking feature film, *The Jazz Singer*.
1928	Walt Disney produces *Plane Crazy*, first Mickey Mouse cartoon.
1929	*Cup of Gold.* *29 October: Crash of New York Stock Exchange. Herbert C. Hoover, Republican,* becomes US President.*
1930	JS marries Carol Henning. JS meets Ed Ricketts, a marine biologist. Frozen foods invented by Clarence Birdseye.
1932	*The Pastures of Heaven.*

104

1933	*To a God Unknown.*
	Increase of dust storms in Great Plains area, eroding topsoil.
	Franklin D. Roosevelt, Democrat, becomes US President.
	Tennessee Valley Authority founded as part of 'New Deal'.
1935	*Tortilla Flat.*
	Refugees from Dust Bowl start migrating to California.
	Roosevelt introduces unemployment and old-age insurance.
1936	*In Dubious Battle.*
	JS writes series on migrant workers for San Francisco News.
1937	*Of Mice and Men* and *The Red Pony.*
	JS travels from Oklahoma to California with migrants.
1938	*The Long Valley.*
1939	*The Grapes of Wrath.*
	Hitler invades Poland – Second World War begins.
	Dust Bowl lessens in severity.
1940	Pulitzer Prize for *Grapes of Wrath.*
	Films of *Grapes of Wrath* and *Of Mice and Men.*
	JS and Ricketts collect sea invertebrates in Gulf of California.
1941	*The Sea of Cortez,* with Ed Ricketts.
	Japan attacks Pearl Harbor, bringing USA into Second World War.
1942	*The Moon is Down*
	Bombs Away for US Air Force.
	Film of *Tortilla Flat.*
	JS divorces Carol Henning.
1943	JS marries Gwyndolyn Conger.

	JS war correspondent in Europe for New York *Herald Tribune*.
1944	Filmscript for Alfred Hitchcock's *Lifeboat*.
	First son, Thomas, born.
1945	*Cannery Row*.
	'The Pearl of the World' published in a women's magazine.
	USA drops nuclear bombs on Japan.
	Second World War ends.
1946	Son John born.
1947	*The Wayward Bus*, novel and film of *The Pearl*.
	JS travels in Russia with photographer Robert Capa.
1948	*A Russian Journal*.
	JS divorces Gwyndolyn.
	Ed Ricketts dies.
1949	William Faulkner awarded Nobel Prize for Literature.
1950	Novel and play of *Burning Bright*.
	Filmscript for *Viva Zapata!*
	JS marries Elaine Scott.
	Start of Korean War.
	Joe McCarthy starts 'witch-hunt' against alleged Communists.
1951	*The Log from the Sea of Cortez*.
1952	*East of Eden*.
	JS writes articles from Europe for *Colliers* magazine.
1953	Elizabeth II crowned Queen of England.
1954	*Sweet Thursday*.
	Hemingway awarded Nobel Prize for Literature.
	McCarthy discredited.
1955	*Pipe Dream* – musical based on *Sweet Thursday*.
	Film of *East of Eden*.
	James Dean, film-star of *East of Eden*, killed in car crash.

1956	Elvis Presley's 'Love Me Tender' becomes a hit.
1957	*The Short Reign of Pippin IV.* Film of *The Wayward Bus.*
1958	*Once There Was A War* – collection of war dispatches.
1960	JS tours USA with dog to prepare for *Travels with Charley.*
1961	*The Winter of Our Discontent.* John F. Kennedy, Democrat, becomes US President. Yuri Gagarin of USSR makes first 'manned' space flight.
1962	*Travels with Charley in Search of America.* John Glenn, American, orbits Earth three times. JS awarded Nobel Prize for Literature.
1963	Kennedy assassinated. Lyndon B. Johnson becomes US President.
1964	USA intervenes directly in Vietnam War, sending troops. JS awarded United States Medal of Freedom.
1965	JS reports from Vietnam for *Newsday.*
1966	*America and Americans.* Ronald Reagan becomes Governor of California.
1968	US Apollo 8 astronauts make first flight around the moon. 20 December: John Steinbeck dies and is buried in Salinas.

Further Reading

The works
Most of Steinbeck's work is available in paperback.

Biography
BENSON, JACKSON J. *The True Adventures of Steinbeck* (Viking, 1984). This biography has been authorised by Steinbeck's family.
BENSON, JACKSON J. *Looking for Steinbeck's Ghost* (University of Oklahoma Press, 1988)
KIERNAN, THOMAS *The Intricate Music. A Biography of John Steinbeck* (Little, Brown and Company, 1979)
STEINBECK, ELAINE and ROBERT WALLSTEN (eds) *Steinbeck: A Life in Letters* (Pan, 1979)
VALJEAN, NELSON *John Steinbeck the Errant Knight, An Intimate Biography of his California Years* (Chronicle Books, 1975)

Background and criticism
DAVIS, ROBERT CON (ed.) *Twentieth Century Interpretations of The Grapes of Wrath. A Collection of Critical Essays* (Prentice-Hall, 1982)
DAVIS, ROBERT MURRAY (ed.) *Steinbeck. A Collection of Critical Essays* (Prentice-Hall, 1972)
FRENCH, WARREN *John Steinbeck* (Twayne, 1961)
FRENCH, WARREN *A Companion to The Grapes of Wrath* (Viking, 1963)
GUTHRIE, WOODY *American Folksong* (Oak Publishers, 1963)
HAYASHI, TETSUMARO *A Study Guide to Steinbeck, Part I* (Scarecrow Press, 1974) and *Part II* (1979)
LANGE, DOROTHEA and PAUL S. TAYLOR *An American Exodus: A Record of Human Erosion* (Yale, 1969)
LAUBER, PATRICIA *Dust Bowl: The Story of Man on the Great Plains* (Coward-McCann, 1958)
LISCA, PETER *The Wide World of John Steinbeck* (Rutgers, 1958)
TIMMERMAN, JOHN H. *John Steinbeck's Fiction, The Aesthetics of the Road Taken* (University of Oklahoma, 1986)
WATT, F. W. *John Steinbeck* (Oliver and Boyd, 1962)

Video material
A BBC television programme, Steinbeck's *Of Mice and Men*, 1980, shows actors in rehearsal for the play and contains an extract from the 1940 feature film. It is available for sale from BBC Home Video.

Many of the films in which Steinbeck was involved are on video.

Bound For Glory is a film (dir. by Hal Ashby, 1976) telling the story of Woody Guthrie (played by David Carradine), the folksinger who left Texas during the 1930s Depression and went to California. He then went 'on the road'. The film has been described as a 'sort of musical Grapes of Wrath' and creates the atmosphere of the period. It is available on video.

Index

Acknowledgements

The author and publishers would like to thank the following for
allowing their illustrations to be reproduced in this book: the
Bettmann Archive 43, 82, 93, 96; Camera Press Ltd 34, 38, 85;
Mary Evans Picture Library 74, 76, 78, 79, 98; The Hemingway
Collection, John F. Kennedy Library 62; the National Film
Archive 48, 52, 58, 64, 66, 69; Peter Newark's Western Americana
20, 23, 24, 26, 30, 31, 44, 55, 61, 68, 75, 87, 89; the Department of
Special Collections and University Archives, Stanford
University Libraries 32, 36, 88, 91; the John Steinbeck Archives,
John Steinbeck Library, Salinas, California 7 (Valley Guild,
courtesy of Steinbeck Library Archives), 9, 10, 11, 12 (Richard
Albee), 15, 16 (Valley Guild), 18, 19, 70, 81, 83, 84 (UPI Photo), 92
(G. Robinson); Topham Picture Library 22, 28, 39, 40, 46, 50, 56,
94. The maps on pages 8 and 45 were drawn by Malcolm S.
Walker.

Extracts from the following works of John Steinbeck are
reprinted by permission of William Heinemann Ltd. The
following works were first published in hardback by William
Heinemann Ltd. *Tortilla Flat*, 1935; *In Dubious Battle*, 1936; *Of
Mice and Men*, 1937; *The Grapes of Wrath*, 1939; *Cannery Row*, 1945;
The Pearl, 1948; *East of Eden*, 1952. Letters are quoted from
Steinbeck: A Life in Letters, edited by Elaine Steinbeck and Robert
Wallsten, published by William Heinemann Ltd. 1975.